To all who will read this book,

Use it to bring you all the good that is destined for you, your family and your home.

Thanking you Kindly.
Happy Feng Shui-ing!

Leanne

What Others Have Said About 2021: The Year of the Yin Golden Ox

"Many go through life not knowing their purpose and thankfully Leanne is not one of them. As soon as she began studying, it was clear that she would become the expert in Feng Shui that she is today.

There are so many facets to this profession that it takes someone of great dedication and knowledge to be able to deliver what is required as successfully as Leanne does.

I have worked with and known Leanne for many years and have a great respect for her tenacity and her relationships that she forms with her clients. Feng Shui is unlike anything else in the marketplace in that it requires a deep understanding of principles and a deep commitment to the ever-changing environment that we see ourselves in. Kudos to you Leanne and here is to many more years of 'setting the intentions' for a better life."

Deanne Scanlan
Journalist and Destination Designer

"Leanne's latest book helped me truly understand how to shift the energy within my home! Her intuitive expertise and encouragement along the way made the whole process so easy and enjoyable! Like having a feng shui master right at my fingertips with every page!"

Madeleine Haydon
Client

2021
The Year of the Yin Golden Ox

Bringing Out the Best in Your Home

Leanne Carius
The Feng Shui Store and More

2021: Year of the Yin Golden Ox

Copyright © 2021 Leanne Carius

Published by Disruptive Publishing

>17 Spencer Avenue
>Deception Bay QLD 4508
>Australia
>www.disruptivepublishing.com.au

All rights reserved. No part of this publication may be reproduced, stored in or introduced into a retrieval system, or transmitted in any form or by any means (including electronic, mechanical, photocopying, recording or otherwise) without the prior written permission of the author. Any person who does any unauthorised act in relation to this publication may be liable for damages.

The information in this book is based on the author's experiences and options. The author disclaims responsibility for any adverse consequences which may result from use of the information obtained herein. Any breaches will be rectified in further editions of the book.

This information is based on the yearly energy only and not with your home energy plan information. Using the Enhancers and tools we have provided here can bring more harmony Qi to your home and workspace. Please chat with Leanne if you would like more information or seek a personal consult. www.fengshuistoreandmore.com

Enquires should be made through email to the author at:
hello@fengshuistoreandmore.com

ISBN:
Print: # 978-0-6450274-3-3
eBook: # ISBN: 978-0-6450274-4-0

Contents

Hello, and Welcome to the Year of the Yin Golden Ox and the 2021 Outlook   11

- The Date for your Chinese New Year Festivities   11
  - 12th February 2021 (Australia)
- Last times we had a Yin Metal Ox Year   11
  - 2009, 1997, 1985, 1973
- What the Golden Ox year has in store for us   12
- The Ox and The Zodiac   14

Foundations   17

- What is Feng Shui in Simple Terms?   17
- What You Must Know   19
- 2021 Blank Bagua Chart for you to copy and use each month   20
- Home Plan   21
- How to find the directions of your home   22
- How to place your Bagua on your home plan   23
- Applying your Bagua to a specific room or area   24

Activated Energy   25

- Yin and Yang   25
- The Feng Shui Realms of Luck   26

Feng Shui for Wellbeing   29

- The Body Bagua   29
- The Family Bagua   31
- The Intention of Belief   33

Cleansing Your Cures and Enhancers — 35

- Enhancers — 35
- Cures — 37
- Saltwater Cures — 39

Checklists for 2021 Preparation — 41

- Preparation Check List for Your Home — 41
  - Mirrors — 42
  - Televisions — 44
  - Sharp Edge Plants — 45
- Preparation Check List for Your Office — 47
- Preparation Check List for Your Thoughts — 49

Feng Shui Afflictions — Error! Bookmark not defined.

- The Areas to be on the watch for — 51
  - Grand Duke Jupiter (Tai Sui) – North-East 22.5 – 37.5 — 52
  - 3 Killings – East 52.5 – 127.5 — 53
  - Sui Po – South West 202.5 – 217.5 – Year Breaker — 54

The Life Aspirations — 55

- The Bagua – Cures and Enhancers — 55
  - SOUTH – Fame, Reputation & Social Connections — 57
  - SOUTH-WEST – Marriage & Relationships — 59
  - WEST – Children, Creativity, & Getting Projects Done — 61
  - NORTH-WEST – Travel, Helpful People & Mentors — 63
  - NORTH – Opportunities & Career Growth — 67
  - NORTH-EAST – Inner Wisdom & Knowing — 69
  - EAST – Family, Relationships & Elders — 71
  - SOUTH-EAST – Your Abundance & Prosperity — 74
  - CENTRE – Tai Ji, the Heart of the Home — 76

Clearing Space Rituals 79

- Crystals 79
- Residual and Ancestry Energy 80
- Smudging 82
- Sacred Bells – Sound Clearing 83

Resources 87

- Kua Number Calculator 87
  - Kua Number Chart 89
  - Kua Chart Specific Meanings and Purpose 90

Afterword 97

A Quick Guide to Me... 99

- Connect with Leanne 101

Hello, and Welcome to the Year of the Yin Golden Ox and the 2021 Outlook

The Date for your Chinese New Year Festivities

The Year *of the Golden Ox* will start on the 12th of February 2021, but for the Feng Shui change, the date will be the 4th of February 2021. We welcome the New Year of the Golden Ox.

For some, you will have noticed an energy shift already and felt the new energy moving into your homes. January is a mix of energy so make sure you take advantage of the excellent energy zones we have in preparation for 2021.

Last times we had a Yin Metal Ox Year

1925, 1937, 1949, 1961, 1973, 1985, 1997, 2009.

We are all looking for a change of Qi for 2021 and this year we are in a Yin year for a start, this resembles more of the feminine energy, so you have the chance of feminine support within all areas of your life including professional and personal.

It is still a metal year, but a softer metal year, being Yin instead of Yang in 2020.

Yin also represents awakening, rediscovery and creating more calm.

2021 is the zodiac of the Ox with the element of earth.

What the Golden Ox Year has in store for us

We have the energy of the Heaven Star that is in the centre of our homes this year. The Heaven Star represents, as its name says, "Heaven Energy". On the positive side, it brings us good fortune and heaven luck. It also represents career, promotions, and success in our endeavours and business advancement, though with a more determined and gentle approach. It brings us support and opportunities for growth and achievement, though we still need to take action when we receive them.

Good for the whole family or those living in your home.

The combined energy in the centre this year is wealth luck; this can be in the way of career or business wealth. The fruits of your labour and good fortune are at play this year.

The Heaven Star is also a gentler energy which can bring a supportive healing Qi to our homes this year.

The Rooster is also very lucky in 2021, and will support the removal of backstabbers and office gossipers.

This year you do not want to become to stuck in your ways and stubborn, or you will find all your energy is getting you nowhere! You need to be a little flexible with the strength of the Ox.

Honest & hardworking is the key to 2021, and the Ox is one of the hardest working animals in the zodiac. This year will require consistent hard work, but the rewards will be bountiful for you.

The Ox is courage and bravery; the Ox protects itself and its tribe, especially its own family and ancestral members, and in particular its lineage.

You are still going to need to make sure you use your "Finding More Me Time Goals" which we talked about in 2020, especially that "Beautiful No" we learnt to say and use.

My Phrase this year is "Just Ask the Question". The Heaven Star is also about support and mentor luck – seek out wiser people who will give you the support you need in 2021. Gather your elders, older mentors and those that you respect to give you guidance and knowledge – you can then apply the hard work, and the world is your oyster.

You want to utilize your networks and mentor luck, make sure you take action where your resources are and watch for resource opportunities that come in from those around you in your industry.

Other traits of the Ox include:

- Trustworthy
- Reliable
- Stubborn – did I mention this? Yes. But it is so important this year!

Have you ever tried to move an ox that does not want to move?

An ox can hold fast and stand strong, but this can also be to your detriment this year, especially while we are recovering from 2020.

You have to take action this year – you have to start with yourself, then others will join you to support and mentor you.

The Ox is a herd animal, so this year is also about connection. You may find that connections that were lost in 2020 that you want to restore will find a way back to you. Let go of the ones that are no longer for your highest good, but keep those that you want to connect with, and keep working on those this year.

The Ox and The Zodiac

This is just a really quick simple guide. There is so much more to how your Zodiac will work this year, and I will be holding webinars to share with you how your year is going to go – be sure to watch our Facebook page or join our newsletter for the dates and information on these.

If you are an Ox, then your ally is the Rat.

You are in Harmony with the Horse and Rooster.

Those that do not need to worry in 2021 are the Tiger, Rabbit, Monkey and Pig.

The Ox is in Clash with the Goat/Sheep this year.

Again, this is just a general list; depending on your own Bazi chart this could be very different for you.

Foundations

What is Feng Shui in Simple Terms?

We cannot manage what we cannot understand, and to understand Feng Shui we need to know a few facts regarding what it is and isn't.

Feng means Wind
Shui means Water

Feng Shui is the flow of wind and water through our environments, with ease and gentleness. There should be no rushing of Qi, as this creates overwhelm; and stagnate Qi builds negative stuck energy within our environments.

It is not religion, magic, or superstition, it is energy – the flow of Harmony.

The best way I can explain energy is to think of the things in our environment that we cannot see – such as gravity. We cannot see it, we cannot touch it, but we are told it is what grounds us; it keeps our feet on the ground and standing upright. Now, for most of us, we would never have questioned that response, we just trust in the answer and reason we have been given.

Well, Feng Shui is like gravity in that it is the energy that grounds our homes, workspaces and selves within our environments. Feng Shui is the unity of environment and energy.

I am a Classical Feng Shui Practitioner using the Flying Stars Method, Compass School, and Form School for this book. If you have not used classical Feng Shui, then please follow the directions carefully so that you do not change anything in your home too quickly, which may confuse your home.

What You Must Know

This is not your home's full Bagua Chart. This is especially important to know.

On the next page is a Flying Star Chart for 2021. This is the Annual Yearly Stars.

Every home will have its own individual chart specific to your home. The chart here goes *over* that chart. You will then have the Annual Monthly Stars that I send in my newsletter every month, which you can find on the Feng Shui Store & More website.

I have included a template there for you to print off each month and write in the energy that is coming into your home. This will give you a quick guide to what areas in your home or business are awesome, and which of those you will want to keep quiet and calm.

Write into it all your cures and enhancer placements for that month. You can also mark the best space for your work connections and where your relationships are the best for that month. Also mark and watch the areas that have unwellness Qi, and the areas you want to avoid. Where do you need to be sure you watch your security, and what Qi are you sleeping on this month? Each month you will have a quick and easy template to work from.

2021: Year of the Yin Golden Ox

THE FENG SHUI STORE & MORE
Year of the Yin Metal Ox 2021

South East	South	South West
East	Tai Jai	West
North East	North	North West

www.fengshuistoreandmore.com

Home Plan

Where can I find it if I do not have a copy?

If you do not have a scaled drawn plan of your home, you can still work with your Bagua, but it will not be as accurate. If you want a plan that is accurate, there are several ways you can get one.

Many local councils have copies of your home plan submitted when your home was built. Most councils today will charge for a copy of your plan, but it is worth having if you want to get the best of your environmental energy chart.

If you cannot get one from your council or you are renting, you could try your local real estate office. Often I have found they are really good sources for getting plans for homes – especially in our area.

If you've got no luck with either of those, then you can draw a plan to scale using graph paper. Simply work out what your ratio will be – meaning a square on your graph paper will equal 1 meter measured of your floor.

You will need to measure each room as accurately as you can to draw up the plan!

The next best thing you can do is to free hand draw your plan as best as you can, and you will find that you can alter it as you get better at working out your space and energy.

How to find the directions of your home

When we are working with your home or office, we are looking for the Facing side of your space. The most Yang energy of your home. For the purposes of placing the Flying Star Chart that we have in this book, all you need to know is the direction of your home's front door, and then the rest will follow.

If, for instance, you know where the sun is rising at your home, then that is the East. If you know where the sun sets, then that is your West.

This is a simple way to start allocating your chart.

Measure out and find the centre point of your home, then place the Bagua centre point onto the centre point of your home plan. Turn the Bagua so that the direction of your front door or the Sunrise or Sunset is in the right position.

Foundations
How to place your Bagua on your home plan

How to place your Bagua on your home plan

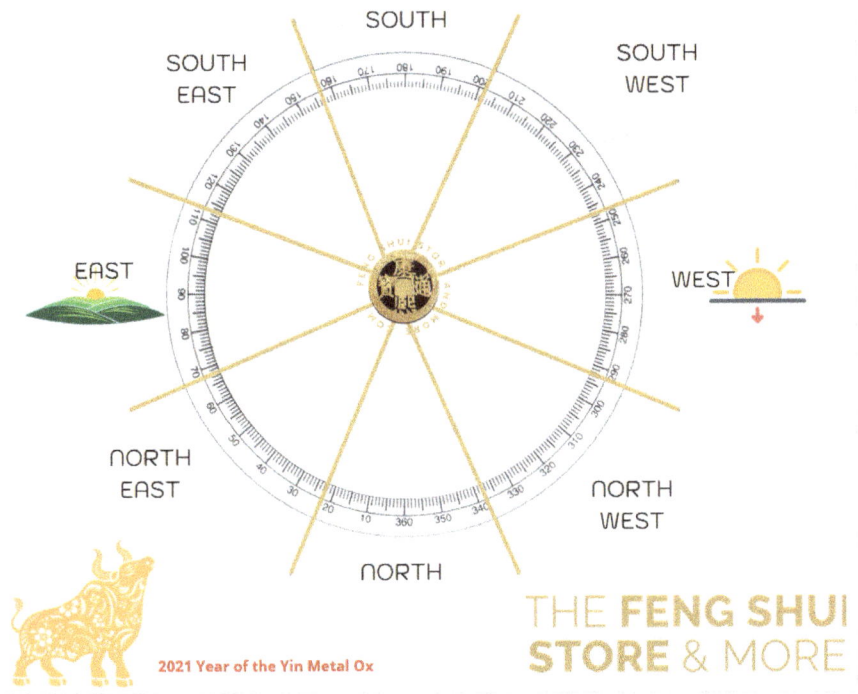

2021 Year of the Yin Metal Ox

Applying your Bagua to a specific room or area

You can also add this template over a single room if you would like to define a room even more. This helps you find enhancer areas within the room. For example, if this is your office, where is the best place to face, and where is your best location to have a conversation?

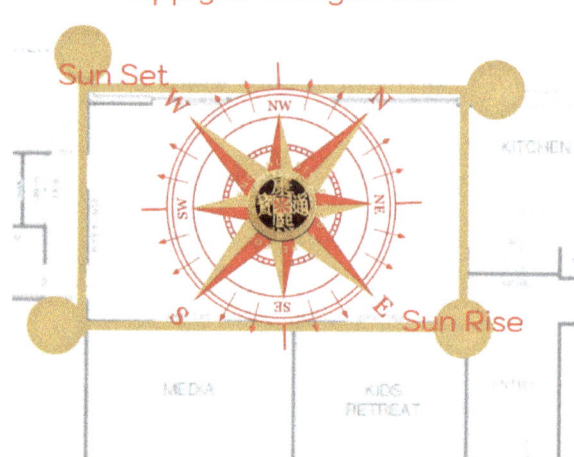

Apply to a single room

Activated Energy

Yin and Yang

The symbol represents a blend of energy:

- o A little positive and negative in everything
- o A little feminine and masculine in everything
- o Light and dark blended to create harmony within our environmental energy
- o Winter through the seasons brings Summer and back to Winter again

They are in complement with each other, each having a touch of the other in their own energy. This is what brings balance to our environments, and harmony to our worlds.

The Feng Shui Realms of Luck

Feng Shui works in the realms of:

- ✓ ***Heaven Luck (Destiny Luck)*** – this is the luck we are born with, and the path that we are travelling due to our destiny – it is our somewhat ordained journey, although I strongly believe that we can alter this journey with some work. Many believe with me that these are the lessons we have asked to learn on this journey. Let's take a minute right now to thank those that have agreed to teach us those lessons and take on that role to help us, and send them love.
- ✓ ***Earth Luck (the ground on which we walk)*** – this is the energy of our place on the earth. Where we live, what time period we are living in, and our home. This luck is the luck many of us can change (not always easily, but it is possible).

✓ *Human Luck (Motivation Luck)* – I love this luck. This is the most important luck in my opinion. This is the luck we can create, change, and move to bring us the most amazing outcomes. This is where becoming intentional is the most important thought process we can have. It is not only our mindset; I always say it is our GET OFF THE COUCH luck – you have total control over this luck, and you can change this luck with the way you think and the way you take action to move forward and in the direction that you choose for your life. This is the luck that we need to motivate us to go for all that we are searching for.

When you are aligned with all the Lucks, then you have clarity in the life you are living.

Feng Shui has been around for many thousands of years, and when you visit the ancient cities and those that follow the traditions, you can see what life is truly about.

It may not mean that their family is living the millionaire lifestyle, but for many it is more than money. It is ABUNDANCE (meaning a very large quantity of something), and that is such a personal word. Yes, for some it will be money, but for others it will be relationships and love. For some (including some of my beautiful clients) it is health – it is more time with loved ones.

We also need to understand that each and every home has a lesson for us, something that we need to learn or experience. You might find that you move a lot, but nothing changes; this is because you are still learning the lesson.

Abundance is the want of more, in so many areas in our lives; be open to wanting more connections than dollars. The dollars will follow your connections.

For me, here is the one mantra I say every morning when I wake:

"My wish is to be healthy,

For if I am healthy, I am wealthy,

For all that I dream within my entire life and,

With the ability to give generously to others."

Feng Shui for Wellbeing

The Body Bagua

Each of the areas of the Bagua reflect a part of your body as well. You can use this quick guide to check the areas that you might be feeling in your body as having a negative energy or Qi that needs to be looked at, cleansed, or cured. Please make sure that you follow up with your doctor if you are not feeling in the best of health.

This Bagua works to give you a simple, quick guide to areas of your home that may need some attention when the energy is showing up negatively in your body.

There is often emotional wellness energy as well; please contact me if you would like to take part in a 30min FREE chat using this link:

calendly.com/thefengshuistoreandmore/feng-shui-qi-chat

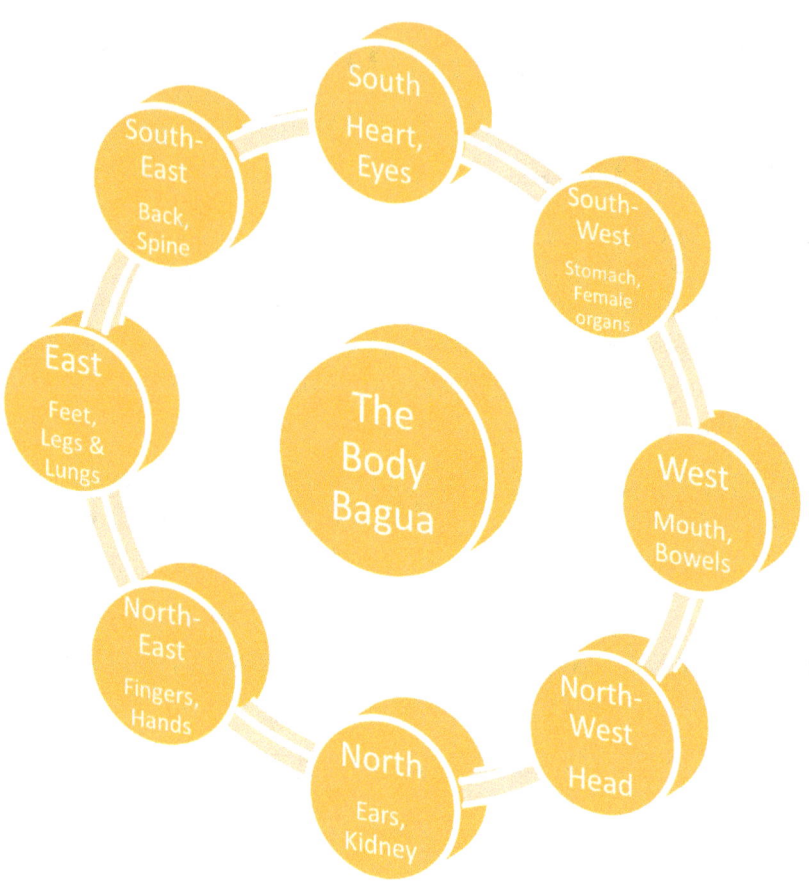

Wellbeing and Self-Care – Ming Gua Sleeping Position. You may want to read this section on your Ming Gua, and your Health directions. This is located on page 82.

Note: if you are ever feeling unwell or think you may need medical attention, please always go to a doctor and ask their advice. I am not a medical expert, nor do I think I can cure you with the information in this book.

The Family Bagua

You can check the energy within your home with a quick check on how everyone in your home is going. Here is a guide to the areas of your home and who they represent.

For example, this year 2021, the energy of unwellness is going to be coming in the North of your home, so if anyone in your family has a bedroom and sleeping in this area then they will need to have cures in place. Your middle son would be a good indicator of how this area is going, as he is represented by the North direction.

Similarly, we will need to watch those who are sleeping in the South East, which has our most disruptive energy. It represents the oldest or only daughter of the family.

You may want to check in with the head man of the home as the energy in the North West could reflect him in 2021. He may want to be careful of sharp objects, especially if he is working with sharp tools or metal. It is also good to watch out for their security as well.

2021: Year of the Yin Golden Ox

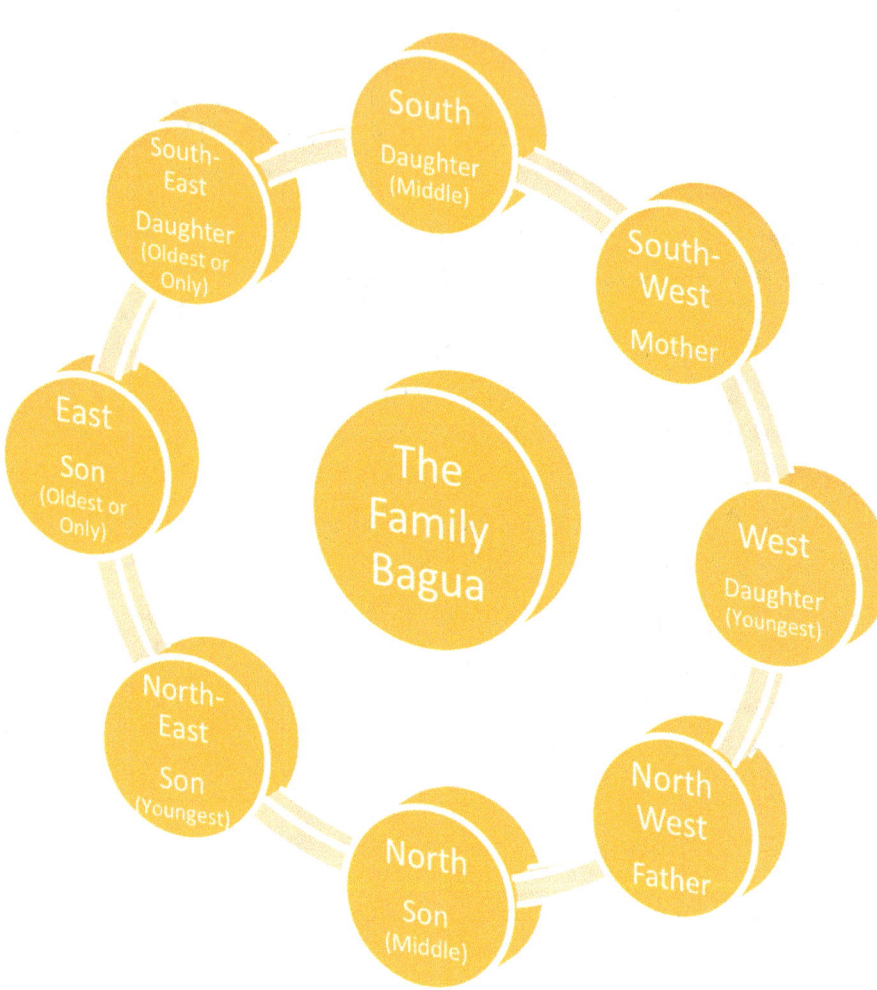

The Intention of Belief

Generally, I find those that ask for my help are often going through one struggle or another and often can be at breaking point. The one important thing that I ask is if you are buying products for you home – BELIEVE that life can be different, and that you can bring about change! Feng Shui products are ancient, and they do work with the energy of your home and yourself – that I can testify to. The most important ingredient is Belief, and how you're thinking when you place your items. Many of the products we have in stock have been used for many hundreds of years and are the staple in the toolbox for Feng Shui Practitioners.

Cleansing Your Cures and Enhancers

Enhancers

Enhancers from the previous year, if they are still looking in good shape, can be reused again this year. Before you place them in their spot for this year there are a few things that you need to do first.

- Take your enhancers and give them a beautiful warm wash. Place them in plenty of sunlight, and a good smudge to reset your intentions will restore them for the new year.
- Check that they are still looking their best with no cracks or breaks. How is their colour?
- Now the most important part – hold them. How do they feel? Does it still bring you the feeling of intention that it was bought for? If the answer is no, then I will always either return it to the earth and say thank you (this is particularly good for coins, crystals and small items), or, if it is larger, then I respectfully say thank you and remove it from my home.
- When your enhancer is ready, check the location it is needed for this year and get ready to place it there. Before you do, think about why you are using this enhancer; what is it going to do for your home or office? What intention are you setting with it? I always find that writing my intentions on a small card can keep them in the forefront of my mind while placing the items.

- Becoming intentional before you place the enhancer down is always important. Take a moment, set the intentions you have thought about, and as you place your item say your intentions (always positive, and energetically sacred).

Cures

Cures – these need to have some special attention, and are the items that you will either already have or are going to place in the areas where negative energy could flow this year.

I never reuse my cure items, and the reason why is this – these items have protected and absorbed all the negative energy that could have come into my home or office over the last 12 months. They are full and they need thanking, and with respect, removal from my home.

Just think for a minute about what they have absorbed.

- Our illness energy
- Our disruptive – sometimes life altering – negative energy
- Our conflict energy
- Our financial and legal negative energy
- Energy that others bring to our space that is negative

Wow! They are our allies of protection, and they are full and exhausted.

If you do have any of these items in bronze or brass and you give them an intentional cleansing and refresh, then you may find that you can use them again. You can do this by giving them a warm wash, plenty of sunlight, and a dose of smudge stick to cleanse.

They do cost dollars, and I am not one for changing for change's sake, but hold them again and just feel how best to move forward.

These are some of the items that you may not want to reuse:

- Bagua Mirrors – our negative energy cure
- Wu Lou – our wellness cure
- String of coins
- 5 Element Pagoda (unless brass and exceptionally good quality)
- Charms and protectors
- Sometimes our bells wear out a little, so check them
- Saltwater Cures – You NEVER want to keep these. Always replace these at the start of each new year.

It is always a good idea during the year to check your cures and make sure that they are still actively working for you. They will be absorbing the energy of the area, so if you feel that the energy is negative, replace them.

Saltwater Cures

Saltwater Cures are especially important, and it is a good idea to always check these to make sure that they have water in them; you may even want to replace these a couple of times during the year if they seem to be worn out. I have placed the instructions for this cure on the Feng Shui Store & More website (www.fengshuistoreandmore.com).

Always make sure you have the right intentions and mindset when placing your cures and enhancers – ***remember what we speak and think, we create.***

I often find some of my lovely clients have a box of cures and enhancers on the ready, so be sure to check them before placing them out for the new year. If you have any enhancers you do not have to place for the year, then store them in a safe space with respect for the next time you need them.

No matter where you are with your journey, you just need to pick a spot and start – this is just your beginning!

Checklists for 2021 Preparation

Preparation Check List for Your Home

Start with your main entrance and work your way through your home and garden, ticking off the important clearing energy items before we begin **The Year of the Golden Ox in 2021.**

Home Ready

- ✓ Can you see clearly from your front entrance to your door, so that Prosperity Qi can flow through and into your home? Is it clear and free of obstacles that would block this Qi?
- ✓ Are there any broken or non-working items in your yard and garden area that will block Qi from flowing?
- ✓ Remove any dying or dead plants from your garden or pots; this is not good for Qi.
- ✓ Is your front door welcoming and clean to welcome the Qi of 2021? Pay particular attention to this if your door is in the NW, SE, West, or SW; this is great Qi flowing.
- ✓ Once inside, make sure you have cleared and removed all the items that you no longer love or use, or are broken.
- ✓ Holidays are a great time to spring clean, but if you are like us and worked all through that time, then take it one day at a time. Choose your battles with your space and start slow, breathe, allow the Qi to support you as you **intentionally clear the spaces.** You have until the 4th of

February for the new year Qi to arrive. I always take the first week of February to do my clean out and freshen our home, ready to welcome the New Feng Shui year.
- ✓ Start at the top of your walls – ceilings, light fittings, and ceiling fans – and work your way down through benches and onto the floors.
- ✓ Make sure you fix up those lights that are needing new bulbs, and any areas that need a little touch up. Fix up any water leaks or leaking taps you may have – that's money down the drain, especially when you are buying water.
- ✓ Remember your office space, especially if you are working from home. Remove what you no longer need so that there is room for your abundance Qi to flow in.
- ✓ Food areas are a big one to go through and remove. How many of us have bought food items we are going to try or experiment with or try a new way of eating, and it is still in our cupboard? Let it go!
- ✓ Ensure that all the items you no longer want in your space have gone where they are needed or have been removed from your home, as this stuck energy needs to go. Now we can really take the next step of **"Becoming Intentional"**.

Mirrors

There are so many thoughts around mirrors and whether they are good in your home or not. I have a couple of general rules I follow and find that they support my home and workspace well, so I stay with them.

Originally, mirrors where made from highly polished stone such as black volcanic glass obsidian. In ancient China,

Checklists for 2021 Preparation
Preparation Check List for Your Home

mirrors were crafted from metal, including tin, copper mixtures, and bronze, which were polished; hence why they became one of the items in the 5 elements toolbox of metal. Even their shape was round, which is the shape we use today for metal. Today, they have a sprayed-on backing, or heated aluminium.

Mirrors create a doubling effect, being that what the mirror reflects, it doubles into your space.

Before placing a mirror, think about:

- ✓ What is it reflecting? This is the most important question. What is being brought into my home or office with the energy of this mirror? Is it a beautiful water course or garden?
- ✓ Placing a mirror near a dining table where you eat and have food can bring the energy of abundance as it can double the look of quantity of food to create the feeling and energy of an abundant home.
- ✓ I have personally found that sometimes a mirror in the wrong space can bring in energy from those that are living next door. I can read energy very easily so this may be a part of why I have to be careful with mirrors, but it is worth the mention to be careful of the energy we are bringing from our neighbours.
- ✓ Another mirror placement area that is debated often with the masters is the bedroom. I go with the theory that being able to see yourself in the mirror when you are in your bed is just downright scary! When I wake in the middle of the night and see someone – oops, that's me in the mirror! Another ancient theory is that our spirit wants to leave our body at night to refresh, travel, and explore, but when

it sees itself in the mirror it gets a fright and drops back down, not to be refreshed. I always say to my clients to experiment with the options and see how the energy feels or changes and to go with that option.

Televisions

This is another one of those debated topics by the masters. I, for one, would never go without my TV in my bedroom. Rob is an early sleeper, and my mind does not slow down as easily. I have tried to stay in the living room, watching the television, but you know what happens then, don't you? Yeah. I fall asleep and have to be woken, or I wake hours later and am ready for another round of motivation as I have had one of my "Wonder Power Naps"!

Really, if it brings you joy and you find it does not mess with the energy of your room, then go for it. I find the timer is an awesome tool on my remote! Set the timer, and I am asleep before my timer goes off.

One point I would make, though, is to choose the shows that will bring you some clarity and calm before sleeping. There are so many amazing programs we can access now with our Apple TV, Google Apps, etc. so I will often choose something that will not give you too many questions or great ideas – although it has happened where I find myself back at my desk creating because I have had a creative breakthrough and the brain is just dumping onto the paper.

I do have one caution for this: if it is getting in the way of your relationships and you are not connecting with your partner, then yeah, the television is possibly the cause, so it may be worth hiding it for a couple of weeks to test it out.

Another idea that was shared with me is to cover the television with pure silk. You can still see through it, but it stops the energy moving through the room. Still out on this one, but I have tried it.

Sharp Edge Plants

I sometimes think you either love these or not. I am not a big fan of sharp pointy things being directed into my energy space, so I always choose not to have these plants around my home. But...

If you do like them and want them, then a couple of things that may help your energy space:

- They are sharp edged, so that reflects similarly to something sharp pointing at you.
- If you have one of these plants in your office, think about where it is pointed. If it is at your back, then just for a minute imagine little daggers coming at your back all day while at your desk. That has got to be uncomfortable. If you have a high-backed chair, then this can help protect your back if you really love your spiky plant.
- Sharp edged plants would not be something I would want to place or have in my North West this year, as the metal energy already heading that way for me, they would just create more sharp energy that I know the head man in our house would not be happy to have this year.
- These plants, when large, can be expensive, so take some time to decide if you want them removed from your garden before rushing in and then being sorry you destroyed

them. It really is a personal choice at the end of the day, and if you are not affected by them – leave them.

Preparation Check List for Your Office

Start with your main entrance and work your way through your office space, ticking off the important clearing energy items before we begin **The Year of the Golden Ox in 2021.**

- ✓ Can you see clearly from your front entrance to your door, so that Prosperity Qi can flow through and into your office? Is it clear and free of obstacles that would block this Qi?
- ✓ In 2021, you want to have your back to the West, facing East. You will not want to be facing the North East.
- ✓ Have a strong wall behind your seat to support you. If this is not possible, then get yourself a high-backed chair and place a small mirror on your desk so that you can see the doorway. This helps to settle you, without you constantly wondering who is going to come through the door and surprise you.
- ✓ You may want to give your desk a clearing also. I always thought I could manage everything as long as no one touched or moved files from my desk, but when I started to take more note of the energy around my desk I realised that if there is no space on my desk, there is no room for Qi to flow.
- ✓ Set yourself up with some great storage spaces. I have a cube shelf near my desk, and I have each cube represent a section of my business. In that section goes my to-do's, what I am working on, and creative new ideas I want to work on – but it is off my desk. I now focus on what is on my desk and only that until it is either completed, or I need to do more research on something or hand to one of my team. Honestly, a complete game changer!

- ✓ Remove old files and items from your previous roles if they no longer serve you. Another thing I did during Covid was to clear out all my files, including electronic files. Everything has now gone. Wow, you say, but what if you need it? Good point, but if I do by any long stretch, then I can Google it again. It is about making a conscious decision to let go, and I did. I had content from 20 years ago! Most of it, if I ever did any work in that field again, is outdated anyway. So, I let it go. I am not saying it is easy. But let it go. Be Brave.
- ✓ There are so many great organising blogs, YouTube channels, and info around today that you can access if you need some inspiration. You may like to join one of my webinars or workshops to learn more or work through with this with more support. Check out my website for our events (www.fengshuistoreandmore.com).

Preparation Check List for Your Thoughts

✓ Remember before you start to ensure that you are using the right words to bring about your intentions for your home.

✓ Are you really ready to create the intentions of the home you so desire? I mean *really* ready?

✓ Ironically, I said in my book last year in 2020: "Let's make this the year that you created change and awesomeness in your home, life and personal spaces!" I have to say how many of us have been changing roles, pivoting our careers, or have had more time to renovate and beautify our homes. It was a tough year, but one that actually got us clearing out the things we no longer need, want or desire.

✓ What is it you are really longing for in 2021? Are you ready to create a home that will support you and those you live with for whatever is for your highest goog?

✓ Okay, let's start now – let's make 2021 the year you enhance the growth and work that you did in 2020, and use this Golden Ox to bring about some greatness for you.

Feng Shui Afflictions

The Areas to be on the watch for

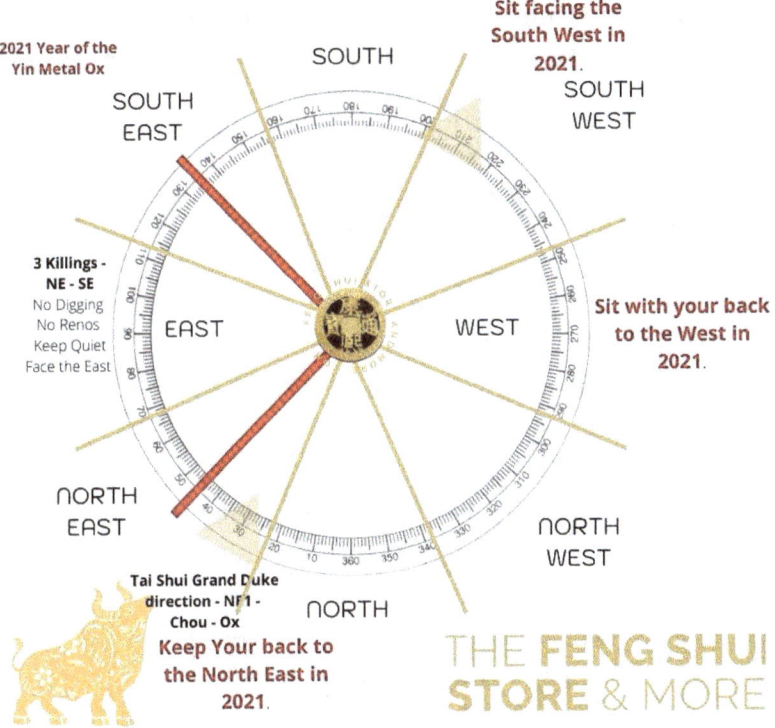

Grand Duke Jupiter (Tai Sui) – North-East 22.5 – 37.5

- The Goat/Sheep is in direct clash in 2021.
- The Dragon and the Dog will need to be cautious also, as they are located near the Grand Duke.
- This year the Ox is the yearly animal, which has support from the Grand Duke, though many masters suggest they also carry the protection medallions.

The Grand Duke's location is governed by the planet Jupiter and its relationship to Earth.

- **What you should not do here:**
  - Face the North East. Check your Kua Number chart; this is to ensure we are not offending the Grand Duke.
  - Have construction, loud noise, or turning soil.
- **What you should you place here:**
  - Pia Yao Fu Dogs, Qi Lin.
  - Protection – Tsi Shen – Pia Yao in the South West, facing North East.
  - Sit with you back to this area.
  - Carry the Tai Sui amulet card.
  - Display the Tai Sui picture.
- **How can you work in this area?**
  - Keep this area quiet, and avoid any construction. If this is your bedroom, office, or gathering space, be sure to add the protectors to support your Qi.

Feng Shui Afflictions
The Areas to be on the watch for

3 Killings – East 52.5 – 127.5

The 3 Killings is the manifestation of three negative energies associated with our wealth, health and relationships. It can bring obstacles, and can mean the loss of someone very close to you.

- Most affected will the Tiger, Rabbit, and Dragon
- Protection:
  - 3 Celestial Guardians, Pia Yao, SWC (saltwater cure), Qi Lin pair
  - You do not want your main rooms (bedrooms, office, gathering areas) here if you can avoid it.
  - You need to face the East this year when sitting at your office desk or any chair. Have your back to the West.

Sui Po – South West 202.5 – 217.5 – Year Breaker

- You want to avoid Construction, conflict, and loud noise here.
- Protectors:
  - Pia Yao or a Study Pagoda (Wen Chang) in the South West.
- Face this direction, with your back to the North East.

The Life Aspirations

The Bagua – Cures and Enhancers

I have placed this chart here for quick reference for the areas that are suitable or even great to use in 2021. Below are the suggestions for your home or office. Please note that with this Bagua, the RED AREAS are GOOD AREAS.

Ancient China always uses RED for ABUNDANCE.

I need to also mention here that this is the BAGUA for the energy we have coming into our homes or offices in 2021.

Your home or office does have a BAGUA of its own also. Sometimes your home Bagua and the Yearly Bagua will have a clash. That being said, you need to place your cures and enhancers carefully and slowly to not disrupt the energy too quickly. If the energy is disrupted too quickly, you cannot find where you need to look further for more clarity around the energy.

Energy can take a couple of weeks to move, but I have found most times that it will happen very quickly.

If for any reason you would like some more help with this, please contact me at hello@fengshuistoreandmore.com.

SOUTH – Fame, Reputation & Social Connections

2021 – Victory Star

How fabulous is this area this year with more wisdom? This is our Nobility energy. There will be no stopping you from accomplishing great things in 2021!

The energy mix here is Wisdom Victory with the multiplier energy.

Our multiplier energy will be a little weakened with the water energy of the Wisdom, but it is still going to be a good space.

Being our Fame and Reputation energy, you may find this a little watered down in 2021, but you have wisdom coming, so that will help you find new ways for you to expand your reputation energy.

Be sure to watch out for those moments when you can achieve your dreams!

Enhancers here are blacks and blues; bring in round bowls of coins and add in your wealth bowls, though you may want to balance that by adding some wood element here also to keep the area of the South working for you.

USE THIS AREA. Expand your connections and put yourself out there with this energy. Make calls here for expanding your networks.

- ✓ Front door – Victory Horse – place a horse here to enhance the energy of the South. The South is the home to the horse, and he is known to bring forth success and movement.
- ✓ Windchimes that are gentle can activate extra energy for you; or, as we have said before, here in Queensland, Australia, we just need to use fans to generate energy – especially in our summer!
- ✓ Carry the Wind Horse keychain with you.
- ✓ Crystal – Clear quartz and amethyst crystal.

If you feel that you are needing some more support in your reputation area, then you may like to bring is a small amount of wood element to enhance your fame and reputation energy. Do this slowly and keep an eye on the energy balance.

The Zodiac benefiting from this energy this year is the Horse.

SOUTH-WEST – Marriage & Relationships

2021 – Quarrelsome Conflict Energy

This area particularly affects the head woman of the home. This is not necessarily the oldest woman, but the woman of the house. Keep this area quiet. Watch for unexpected conflict and challenges.

You will need to be careful of words this year, and quarrels that you find yourself involved in.

Mums with children at home, be careful of short tempers this year. Have an exit strategy ready for when those days may become a little more than you can handle.

Stay calm, and do not have any important conversations in this space. Conversations that escalate can result in legal issues for those working in this area, so best to avoid this area for your office this year.

Relationships may be a little more challenging, and those that are married may need to find a calmer way to speak and approach each other this year.

If married, keep your pair of Mandarin Ducks in this space side by side travelling on the same path to support unison in your relationship.

Be cautious if you have your front door facing this way, or a bedroom or office in this location.

- ✓ Add a little red or fire energy here this year to calm the quarrelsome Qi; Quan Yin or our Serenity Buddha will also assist with creating peace.
- ✓ Your Magic Flame Keyring will be awesome here, and the Magic Flame Plague.
- ✓ Bring your Fu Lu Shou into this zone of your home if it's a living room or family room.
- ✓ Reduce the number of plants and water you have in this area.
- ✓ Reduce the water elements in this area.
- ✓ You can use red colours in your mats, rugs, towels, and throws.
- ✓ Add a rooster statue on your office desk to support the energy and reduce the backstabbing, especially if you have an office woman.
- ✓ Bring in your elephant of protection.
- ✓ You will have the Sui Po in this area for 2021.
- ✓ Avoid renovations and loud noises here.
- ✓ Place a bell on the door or at the entrance to this area to break the Qi as you enter.

PLACE YOUR PI YAO IN THIS AREA FACING THE NORTH-EAST, TO APPEASE THE GRAND DUKE.

- ✓ Crystal – Amethyst, rose quartz, turquoise or clear quartz energy is also good here this year.

The Zodiacs most influenced by this energy this year are the Monkey and Goat. Monkey, you have a whole heap of great energy headed your way this year, so make the most of the positive year. Goat people – just be cautious.

The Life Aspirations
The Bagua – Cures and Enhancers

WEST – Children, Creativity, & Getting Projects Done

2021 – Wealth, Prosperity & Abundance

What a great energy in 2021!

Use this area for both business and important planning. We are in Period 8 until 2023, so this is very auspicious energy for us here.

You may find that your children will be creating extra money this year, and if you are creative, start using your talent to bring in that extra abundance.

Be careful not to bring in too many metal items this year, but you can certainly use items such as your ingots, wealth bowls (ones made from pottery are very good this year) and metal coins.

- ✓ Any of your money enhancers, like Buddha and his money bags and ingots.
- ✓ Tsi Shen, the money god.
- ✓ Monkey on horseback.
- ✓ Wealth Ox on coins.
- ✓ A Victory Horse here will bring movement forward.
- ✓ A touch of red colour in this area will bring the energy of the 8 here a little more to life.
- ✓ Use this area, and add light to the space.
- ✓ If you need some help in getting your ideas created, then carry the Ruji keyring or place Ruji on your desk.

- ✓ Crystal – Tiger's eye, shungite, smoky quartz, fluorite, citrine.

Zodiac is the Rooster. Find a friend or colleague who is a Rooster, and they will support the reduction of gossip and backstabbing energy this year. Great to have someone like this in your office.

NORTH-WEST – Travel, Helpful People & Mentors

2021 – Robbery and Financial Loss Energy

Fighting, challenges, lawsuits and backstabbing, just to name a few of the negative energies here for 2021; this is going to create some cutting Qi for many of us, especially for the patriarch of the family.

We could find conflict, legal issues, and disputes, so be sure to reduce the metal energy that is in this space.

There is a good chance that you can find wealth through competition if you follow the opportunities, though you are going to have to be on your game, especially for men.

As always though, we do have some positive energy that can used by some of you – if you are someone who deals in legal issues and law courts, then this energy could very well play in your favour.

Be cautious of travel in the north-west direction, and be sure to carry your Blue Rhino keyring with you when you do travel this year.

North-west represents the head man of the family, so be sure the man of your home takes care of themselves and their energy.

As I mentioned at the start of this book, we need to watch out for our male bosses, managers, and those that rule, including heads of state. This energy is going to cause distrust, fighting, and loss.

If you are a man with a team under you, then you need to be cautious that you do not become dictatorial. Similarly, if your leader or boss is a man, you may want to choose the right time and perfect place for those conversations that need to be had when operating in a business or corporation. The authority energy here is too strong this year and can cause some real issues.

- Male bosses, executives and business owners, you may want to get yourself our Guan Yu – Warrior – Protector and Guardian. Also known as Kuan Kong and Guan Gong.
- You may want to wear our OM PEDI pendant or have it close by for those moments you need to stop and take a moment. Turn the pendant until you have found some calm.

This energy can also cause betrayal luck, so be conscious of how you are handling others around you. If you have an office in this location, you need to be extra cautious.

- ✓ You can bring in the water element to reduce the Qi in this space – things like blue and black colours or water items such as water itself (but not moving water; simply a large bowl of water outside). You can also add a clear vase of water here with 3 Bamboo (fresh) stems to reduce the energy of loss.
- ✓ Add your 3 bamboo in a vase of water only to this area, especially if this is an office on your desk at work.
- ✓ Add the Blue Rhino to this space, or an Elephant with a raised trunk for protection.

The Life Aspirations
The Bagua – Cures and Enhancers

- ✓ Keep an eye on the security of your home in this area, and check you have good locks on your windows and doors if away.
- ✓ Be careful of your finances, and be sure to watch for signs such as:
    - the wrong change given
    - charges over a quoted price
    - misplacement of your wallet or purse
    - losing your credit card
    - extra transactions on your statement that you did not add yourself
- ✓ As always, never put any fire element or red colour in this space.
- ✓ Be cautious if you have a wood stove or fireplace here; this includes fire pits and BBQs in your outdoor area in this zone.
- ✓ Electric stoves are not as strong in the fire element, but gas stoves are a flame and should be avoided.

If your stove, oven, or fireplace is located in this space, then add a bowl of water to the area. If this is difficult, it could simply be a picture of water, though this is not as effective as water itself. Another cure is said to be the energy of earth to reduce the fire element.

This energy is also a strong Qi for fire, so be sure to check and make sure you watch anything that is plugged in for long periods of time like computers, iPads, or phones charging.

NOW – this year we have to ask. We need to ask for support of those wiser than us and of our elders, so be sure to place your intentions in this space and ask for the help you need in 2021.

For travel luck:

- ✓ Be cautious of travel in 2021, particularly if you are travelling North West.
- ✓ Placing a bowl of international money (notes, not the coins this year) here always works well.
- ✓ Bring in a globe of the world, and mark your travel places. I flag mine with the dates as well. Remember, if the borders are not open yet, you can still find plenty of places to explore and reconnect with just outside your own front door.

The best travel is North-East and West in 2021.

The Zodiacs for this area are the Dog and Pig. Just be careful. You will have a better year than 2020, but you need to stay cautious and observant and watch the men around you – do not get drawn into that energy.

NORTH – Opportunities & Career Growth

2021 – Negative wellness energy

Our negative wellness energy finds itself in the North for 2021, and this is going to help lessen the energy this year, compared to 2020 when it was in our fiery South.

If you have an office located in this space, you could find some setbacks within your career growth. There may not be as many opportunities for you this year, though the more action we take the more we find they will appear for us. If you do have an office here, add in some metal element to increase your career luck.

Look out for fatigue and lack of energy. Reduce this with:

- ✓ A Wu Luo.
- ✓ No red or fire energy.
- ✓ Add a medicine Buddha in gold or bronze colours.
- ✓ Ivory Medicine are also good in this area.
- ✓ Green Tara is for removing obstacles.
- ✓ A bell on the entrance here to break the Qi as you enter this space.

Our thoughts create emotional wellness let go of fear and negativity.

Be cautious if you have a Bedroom in this space particularly if someone is currently already unwell or have a compromised health issue. You need to ensure you have cures in place if your front door is in this space as well.

- ✓ Crystal – Black onyx – a protective warrior stone bringing calm to our thoughts. Agate. My favourite is black tourmaline.

The Zodiac of the Rat, and the middle son, need to be more careful of their health in 2021.

NORTH-EAST – Inner Wisdom & Knowing

Grand Duke 22.5 – 37.5

2021 – Future money & the multiplier

A very auspicious energy in 2021.

The fire element is here this year, and represents our inner wisdom and knowing.

We also have the Sum of Ten, which is our completion combination. Perfect for getting things finalised. Make use of this energy on projects you have been procrastinating on and avoiding. You can also use this energy to complete anything that was not fully removed or let go of in 2020.

Enjoy this space if you have your front door located here. If your bedroom is located here, then make use of this serene energy. It's excellent for a meditation space, journaling, and self-awareness discovery. It would make a divine retreat space in your home.

For protection against the Grand Duke in this area in 2021, it is advised to not be facing the North East. Place your Pi Yao in the Southwest facing the North East.

- ✓ You want to keep this area quiet, no loud noise. No building or renovating in this area.

The energy also represents our future investments and money income, so your Year of the Ox statue would be awesome here, especially with his coin base.

- ✓ Crystal – Amazonite – for speakers and performers, this crystal is for inspiration and clarity. For children you can use clear quartz, rose quartz and black tourmaline.

The Zodiacs benefiting from this area are the Ox and Tiger. The youngest son is also going to benefit from this energy this year.

EAST – Family, Relationships & Elders

52.5 – 127.5 (3 Killings & Sui Po)

2021 – A better year for communication

The energy of study, learning, writing, and knowledge, and yes – romance. Keep this area quiet. Watch for unexpected conflicts and changes.

After the Emperor's negative Qi in 2020, we have a wonderful change in 2021. This is a great area for students, learners, writers, and creatives, and an excellent space for student desks. **Add an Education Tower** to their study desks for bonus support in learning.

This is an excellent office space in 2021, particularly for creatives. If you're writing a book this year, find a space here and get down to doing it.

Just be cautious that there is not too much energy here, as this can create some extra Qi around couples already in a relationship. If you are looking for romance though, this is the area to put your intentions and make it happen. Marriage luck is available and is excellent for supporting those already in a relationship.

Place enhancers such as:

- ✓ A horse for moving forward.
- ✓ Your Chinese writing tools and creative tools.
- ✓ Positive items that reflect new opportunities and growth, like the Phoenix.

- ✓ Bring your Dragon in here for protection and success, or place it on your desk. Dragons love the East, and are right at home here.
- ✓ Rabbits carrying the 3 Celestial Keyrings to protect against the 3 Killings.

Peach blossom and romance energy is floating in this space, also and brings a strong energy. Check out our resources page (www.fengshuistoreandmore.com) to find out what is your peach blossom, and place that animal here to boost your romance and business luck.

- ✓ Use this area!
- ✓ Place your Mandarin Ducks here. Remember not to have them facing each other – they should be side by side, travelling on the same journey, for longevity.
- ✓ If you require a little more balance between your Yin and Yang energy, then the Phoenix and Dragon Hanger is a must.
- ✓ If you have your bedroom here, you could add a little extra to the doorknob with a Double Happiness Hanger or our Tantric Cheeky Boy.

If you find this energy if a little overwhelming with the double wood element, then bring in a touch of fire element colour to the area.

- I would avoid candles and flames in this space, as they are very strong in the fire element.

We have the energy of THE THREE KILLINGS here in the Year of the Ox. You can find more details on this on page 49.

- ✓ Crystal – Rose quartz, pink tourmaline, and ruby for vitality.

The Zodiac for here is the Rabbit – it's a much better year for you this year. This area also affects the eldest son the most.

SOUTH-EAST – Your Abundance & Prosperity

Emperor's Qi – Disruptive Negative energy

This energy creates challenges that can seem impossible to overcome. Do not use this area for business or sensitive projects in 2021.

The Southeast is your abundance, though this year we have the Emperor's Qi here, which can be extremely negative. In 2021, however, we will find this energy is not as strong as it has been previously due to the metal energy of the South East.

- ✓ Reduce this energy by not placing fires or reds here.
- ✓ Bring in yellows, golds, and metal shapes and materials to calm this area.
- ✓ Do not do renovations in this area; make sure it is quiet.
- ✓ Place your 5-Element Pagoda here; make sure you lock up the earth from the South East. This can be from your own yard or from the yard of someone you aspire to or value in your growth and prosperity. This must be done before the 4th of February 2021; after this date, just leave it empty. You can also place your 6 metal auspicious coins in the top dome.
- ✓ 6 coins and yellow string.
- ✓ Use your Fu Lu Shou for protection over your home and family.
- ✓ Carry the 5-Element Pagoda Keyring.

✓ Place a Bagua mirror outside here.
✓ Add a Chiming clock here (make sure it is working).
✓ A 6-rod metal windchime outside in this area, or a metal bell on the door, will help to break the Qi when the door is opened or closed to disperse the energy.

Be cautious if you have your front door facing this way, or a bedroom or office in this location.

- South-East – Secondary Wealth and Abundance

When you support yourself as being abundant – such as in the areas of health, wealth and happiness – you will see the opportunities that make you abundant.

✓ Crystal – Black tourmaline is an energy shield providing protection both from energy coming into our home, and from our own thoughts. With love, it sends the energy back outside of you and your home.

The Zodiacs experiencing this energy are the Dragon and the Snake – you may want to carry the 5-Element Pagoda with you. The Dragon has a good year coming in general, though.

CENTRE – Tai Ji, the Heart of the Home

2021 – The Heaven Luck Energy

In 2021, this is great energy. This energy is around your career and advancement. It is also known as the military star.

The Heavenly Star brings us more mentors and helpful people this year, and they will be active in your professional standing and achievements. This is an energy of opportunity and growth.

✓ Metal represents wealth, including auspicious coins, gold ingots, and wealth bowls.

The Tai Ji represents the Heart of the Home, and this is where we find the lessons that a home is bringing to us. Ever had that feeling like you are going from one house to the next, but they all end up feeling similar and nothing is changing? Lessons from your home are for you to learn and grow from; they are there to teach us something that we need to be aware of. It could be:

- Money locks
- Health locks
- Relationship locks

All these clues are found in the centre of your home.

A question we get asked a lot is how big is this area in my home? And the answer is always, "that depends" – so find yourself a good Feng Shui practitioner to support you in finding the lesson from your home and working out how large an area it takes up.

The earth energy of your Tai Ji will help to enhance the energy of the metal energy we have coming in here this year.

Use this area when you are applying for a career move or advancement.

Strong careers are represented here, so be sure to watch for opportunities in your chosen career path in 2021.

- ✓ Again, your Horse here will have you moving successfully forward.
- ✓ Avoid candles and strong fire elements this year, as these will weaken the positive Qi.

Some enhancers include adding extra bowls of coins.

Tsi Shen will stand guard and bring your success and achievements into your home for all living in your space here. This is an excellent area for any statues or objects that reflect abundance for you.

- ✓ Crystal – Fluorite, clear quartz for clarity, green aventurine.

Clearing Space Rituals

This is the really important area where we get to take care of the energy we surround ourselves with; our final clearing and cleansing process. When I work with my clients, we always finish off with this process.

Begin Somewhere! If this all feels too much and you are not sure that it is for you, then choose one cleansing ritual and just start there. When you are ready, you will find your path. Simply Begin...

Crystals

I am sure most of you have a good understanding of how to cleanse your crystals, but if you are not familiar then here are some ways to prepare your crystals for use.

- Be sure that when you get them home, you either:
  - Place in the moonlight, sunlight or a warm bath of water.
  - Dry them – this can be done in the sunlight.
  - Take them into your hands and give them your intentions.
- Set intentions for your crystals. This is really important. Be sure that you:
  - Have taken the time to get to know your crystal, what its purpose is, why you chose it.
  - Are sure that it is in the positive to start with.
  - Are clear about what you are setting and why you are setting it.

- Hold it in your clean hands, mediate on it and on your intentions, then draw in a breath of air and exhale that onto your crystal – all your intentions, and all that is for your highest good. Do this 3 times.
  - Once complete, place your crystals around your home in the places they are most reflective of and say, "Thank you", or "Namaste".

Residual and Ancestry Energy

Over the years, furniture and ancestor heirlooms – second-hand items and things received from loved ones – have been the biggest challenge for many of my clients. How to handle them is such a personal thing, but I will share with you some thoughts to consider.

  - First and foremost – do you love it? Is it something that brings you immense joy and pleasure when you touch it or hold it? Do you have fond memories of it? For those of you who know me, you will know the story of my Grandmother's piano. It does not work well, and it is huge, old, and takes up a lot of space. I have been encouraged for years to give it away. Why I do not is simple – I just cannot! I have sat with it and thought about why this connection is so strong, and each time I do I just get the beautiful memory of my grandmother. I see how hard she worked to be able to afford this beautiful piano in its day, and I have the room to keep it. So, I do!
  - Ask yourself why you are keeping the item. If you feel, like I mentioned above, that you have the room and space for Qi to flow around the items, then love them and hold them. If for some reason you are struggling with space,

or you feel overwhelm at it being in your home, then think again on why you are keeping it.
- If you need some help to move it on, then get a 30 min FREE chat with me and we can work you through letting it go (you can find this at the end of this chapter).

If you have a sense that you have someone in the house with you, there are three things this could be:

- This is one of your loved ones who are here to watch you and guide you. When you sit quietly, ask them to give you a huge hug, and you will feel the air around you tighten, and a sense of warmth surround you. Sit in this and just share the love.

- This is someone your child senses, sees or feels in your home. Often, again, this is someone who is watching over your child and protecting them. I have had several of my grandchildren share their stories of having someone visit them. My granddaughter was actually playing "round and round the garden" on her hands with her little spirit boy in the back of the car one day. Children are so open to the energy around them. As with my grandchildren, it is not something that we all encourage or discourage, but we do have open and honest conversations around those who have died and gone before us and how we can still connect and communicate with them. This is so important, especially if they have a connection to that person and remember them. They are no different to us when it comes to suddenly just missing someone and feeling sad. One of my little grandsons often chats to me

about my Dad, and I have absolute faith that Dad is popping in to check on him when he is sleeping.
- This is someone attached to the home, or attached to you that you have brought into your home. This is different; this is certainly an energy that feels heavy and stifled. Often with my clients, it is someone who just needs some encouragement to leave the earthly plane, as they have just gotten a little lost. Similarly, you might have a piece of furniture that you have brought home which has a residual energy; if so, give it a really good cleanse and a smudge to remove the energy. It is worth speaking to someone who can support you if you feel the energy is dense and heavy and your efforts to smudge and cleanse do not seem to be working.

If at any time you are unsure and feel that you would like some support with an energy within your home, please contact me and I would be happy to chat with you on how we can work together to clear the energy.

Once your spring clean is done, open your doorways and your home.

Smudging

Start with a good smudge of your home. Remember to use your positive words while smudging to create the intentions of the home you are after for 2021. I always use: **"may my home be healthy and wealthy, and all those that live, visit, and share here enjoy the same energy."** I am a big believer in "without health, you cannot have wealth". Please make sure that if you are using Palo Wood that it is responsibly harvested. White sage is excellent, but it makes my nose itchy so I use Basilica or our White Sage clearing spray instead.

Sacred Bells – Sound Clearing

Clearing with the sound of bells and windchimes can be a great way to move any stuck energy, especially in corners or in rooms that are not used often. You will find that if you set your intentions and are in tune to the energy of your home, your bells will just not ring; it is hard to believe, but they just will not sound when energy is stuck. Stay in that spot until you hear your bells clearly.

Pay particular attention to your front and back doorways, and if you have a garage adjoined to your home, remember to do that as well as the large garage doors. Do not forget your office – under the desk in the draws, and where your money is kept.

Under beds is another area where energy can sit and stagnate. Pay particular attention to bedrooms in the South-East, North, North-West, and South-West this year.

Hallways are also where energy and Qi are likely to hover, so make sure you clear them also.

Put on your favourite piece of slow breath music and take yourself to that long-drawn bath you have ready for yourself – wash the last of the unwanted Qi away and put on those fresh clothes you had, settle in for a relaxing tea or wine (no judgement here – you've earnt it!). Enjoy this moment in the new energy.

✓ Make your last tick in this box – "My home is becoming the intention I create from within."

Clearing Space Rituals
Sacred Bells – Sound Clearing

If you would like a clearing and cleansing session, please connect with me! I would be happy to chat more with you on what we do and the dates I have available. Here is the link to a FREE 30min chat:

calendly.com/thefengshuistoreandmore/feng-shui-qi-chat

Resources

Kua Number Calculator

This is one of the most important things for communication this year. Your Kua number (also known as the Ming Gua number) is a tool that gives you the right directions you need to be facing for important meetings, conversations and relationships and your health. It's your "Power Seat".

Calculating your Kua

For Women:

1. Add the last two numbers of your birth year together, and bring it to a single digit.
2. Add 5 to your single digit (if you were born after 2000, add 6 instead).
3. Add the resulting number together again to form another single digit.
4. This is your Kua number!

For Men:

1. Add the last two numbers of your birth year together, and bring it to a single digit.
2. Deduct your single digit from 10 (if you are born after 2000, deduct it from 9 instead).
3. This is your Kua number!

For Example:

If I was a woman born in 1971:

1. Add the last two numbers of the year of birth and bring it to a single digit:

   $$7 + 1 = 8$$

2. Add 5 to your single digit:

   $$8 + 5 = 13$$

3. Add the resulting number together again to form another single digit:

   $$1 + 3 = 4$$

4. #4 is your Kua number!

If I was a man born in 1942:

1. Add the last two numbers of your birth year together, and bring it to a single digit:

   $$4 + 2 = 6$$

2. Deduct your single digit from 10:

   $$10 - 6 = 4$$

3. #4 is your Kua number!

NOTE: *be aware of it that if your birthday date is before the February date of Chinese New Year, in that year your birth year will move to the earlier year (for example: 30th of January 1964 becomes 1963).*

DO NOT FACE the North-East this year if your Kua number is one of these directions due to the Grand Duke energy there this year.

Resources
Kua Number Calculator

Kua Number Chart

	SUCCESS	HEALTH	LOVE	PERSONAL GROWTH	UNLCKY 1	UNLUCKY 2	UNLUCKY 3	UNLUCKY 4
KUA 1	South East	East	South	North	West	North East	North West	South West
KUA 2	North East	West	North West	South West	East	South East	South	North
KUA 3	South	North	South East	East	South West	North West	North East	West
KUA 4	North	South	East	South East	North West	South West	West	North East
KUA 5		Men Use Kua 2		Women use Kua 8				
KUA 6	West	North East	South West	North West	South East	East	North	South
KUA 7	North West	South West	North East	West	North	South	South East	East
KUA 8	South West	North West	West	North East	South	North	East	South East
KUA 9	East	South East	North	South	North East	West	South West	North West

Now, take your directions and circle your area in each section. Take a photo of your chart and keep it with you wherever you are. You can go to this link for more information about how to calculate your chart:

https://fengshuistoreandmore.com/how-to-calculate-your-kua-number-power-seat/

Kua Chart Specific Meanings and Purpose

SUCCESS – My Power Seat

This is the direction you need to be facing.

This is an awesome tool, especially for your home or work office. Look at where your desk is positioned – which direction you are facing? You may need to move your chair slightly; you can use any of the other directions to give you your most positive direction if your Power Seat direction is not possible. Use it in board rooms, or when just having a conversation with a client or partner where you need to have success on your side.

You will use this direction for things such as:

- ✓ Important meetings
- ✓ Financial meetings
- ✓ Employment and career meetings
- ✓ Projects where you need a win
- ✓ Securing new client work
- ✓ Anything that is associated with your business and personal success

Anything that you define in your life that you need to be successful at, then this is the direction for you at that time.

HEALTH & WELLBEING – My Wellness Seat

This is the direction that you use for sleep. You should have the crown (top) of your head towards this direction while you are sleeping. A way to do this is by having the head of your bed against the wall (solid wall preferable) in this direction of the house. This is our restoration of wellbeing direction.

One question I get asked so often is – "What if my partner and I have different directions?" Well, I always believe that the person who is most important in your family, as in they are bringing the bacon home or they are the major contributor to the home, should have their direction first. Now let me say here before you get a little worried that you do not count in this process – you do! – but who do you feel is the one who is going to bring the family the most drama if they are not able to contribute?

In my home, we are lucky that we have both got a metal element number, but I would put Rob before me because he has a much more labour-intensive role than I do, so he needs the great health and energy to do that role more than I do.

Do not let the direction become a big matter for you; it is simply working out a wholesome approach to who needs the support. You can always change to give everyone some good energy!

LOVE – My Connection Seat

Oh, this is the one I do love the most, and the one I check in on often! This is the direction you need to be facing for love.

It is not just about our partner love, but the relationships we have with many people.

You can use this direction for:

- ✓ Speaking to those we have an intense, deep affection for
- ✓ Speaking to those that you love, such as partners (make sure they are facing their best love direction as well)
- ✓ Speaking to family members – this is always a good direction for those hard to have conversations
- ✓ Speaking to those we have an interest with
- ✓ Speaking with those we work with – it brings the conversation from a deeper place for you – more centred and controlled
- ✓ Those hard to have conversations with anyone, really – this will bring us in from a more centred and controlled conversation space

PERSONAL GROWTH – My Wisdom Seat

Love this one too. This is my profoundly wise direction of self.

This is about reaching your full potential, whether that be in knowledge, personal, emotional, or physical. It can even be when we want to take our intentions and soul to the next level. This is a great space to face while meditating, or working in your journal. This brings me my sensibility and saneness.

This is the direction you need to be facing for:

- ✓ Undertaking anything that involves your knowledge and personal growth
- ✓ Office spaces
- ✓ When you are studying
- ✓ When you need some sound judgement on anything
- ✓ Meditating and journaling
- ✓ Attending workshops and spaces of new learnings
- ✓ Our children who are at school – great if they can face this direction while learning
- ✓ Children's study areas within the home

UNLUCKY DIRECTIONS – My Less Desirable for my Greater Good Seat

As with everything in Feng Shui, there is always going to be the Yin/Yang, Positive/Negative energy, and we have that with our directions as well.

Ancient Chinese philosophy says that these directions can bring extreme misfortune – I like to focus on the positive ones at the top and do my best to be in those directions. Unlucky are the directions that I always say are less desirable for our greater good.

Let's face it – we cannot always get the best spot. But a little further on I have given some tips on how I deal with that.

I find that if I am facing any of these, I can often:

- ✓ Feel uncomfortable – unsure of myself or my space
- ✓ Feel I am not in my power space
- ✓ Feel less confident in the words I want to speak with and use, and can often create a situation with those words that I am sorry for later
- ✓ Know that the direction I am facing is extremely negative, and I need to leave it
- ✓ Feel disempowered and lacking

Now, while these directions can put me off my game, I have a method that will get me back on point and into the game quickly! I can do this even in a public space, so these are great for meetings.

Resources
Kua Number Calculator

- ✓ Take a minute and just centre yourself
- ✓ Take a deep breath right down into your belly and slowly release it
- ✓ Carry a clear quartz crystal in my pocket, and take it in my hand while centring myself
- ✓ Qigong power lifter – this is a great tool for building your energy power centre. Sit in a chair and breathe calmly. You then take your hands and place your fingertips together, so that the tips are just touching. Place hands in front of your stomach. While you are breathing in take your hands apart slowly and follow the intention of building energy, then on the out breath bring your fingertips back together again. Do this several times until you feel centred and calm

Tips on Getting My Directions

I know them off by heart, and you will get to know them this way also.

I always get to my meetings early so that I can get out my compass (yeah, I carry one with me everywhere) and find my Power Seat. You will get to know the feeling with this seat, and find that after time you will just know the direction you need to sit in.

When planning to have the hard conversations, that is also what I do – I plan so that I can make sure that many of those around the table are also facing their best directions.

As I said earlier, Rob gets the Health direction at home, but when I am travelling – which I do a lot – I always make sure I get myself in *my* directions. This can mean sleeping across the bed, which I have done when away on my own and needing to have my best "ME" present the next day.

I Trust that things will be as they are. I always know that the universe has my back; nothing that is meant for me will go past me, and if it does, it was not meant for me; I need to get ready, because something better is about to arrive.

Afterword

Life is about bringing in the things we love and desire.

There is no denying that it can bring us challenges at times, be that money, health, or love, but it is the energy we sit in that changes the way we look at those challenges.

Opportunities are everywhere, but when we assume that the doorway is closed and cannot see how to open that new doorway of opportunities, then we miss that moment. It is gone.

I know you can do this! You've got it. Just take it one moment at a time, start at the start, begin at the beginning. I have left you links to so many resources to make this journey easy for you, and 2021 is going to be seeing you in AWESOMENESS.

It is not Magic, it is called Harmony.

Happy Feng Shui-ing!

Leanne

A Quick Guide to Me...

I am:

❖ A Wife to the most amazing man for over 37 years.

❖ A Mother to 4 independent, remarkably successful children.

❖ A Mother-in-law to their beautiful partners.

❖ A Grandmother to 5 beautiful joys.

❖ From an extremely large family of over 40 members, and the eldest of my sibling tribe.

I continue to connect to a beautiful group of Empowered Women – Empowering each other to join the journey to inner wisdom and success, always supporting each other.

I have an understanding of energy that keeps me on my toes and searching for new and creative ways to bring that energy to others.

I shake up your environment with a blend of Traditional Eastern Philosophies and the science of the modern Western Mindset, finding what works for you and your external and internal Qi energy.

With thanks, some say that I am not only an accredited classically trained Feng Shui Practitioner, but a gifted Mindset Champion, Qi Aligner and Changer, with an incredible understanding of human behaviour, environment, and energy.

I have worked with many business owners, helping them to find a living and working space where their environmental energy achieves their own definition of success.

I am also a Retreat Facilitator to feed your soul and allow inner wisdom to guide you to find "Certainty of Self". Traveling with my retreat work to experience the Shambalas of Australia and Internationally is one of my greatest joys …

… For the culture,
… The experience,
… The diversity of people you can connect with, and
… The chance to simply be generous to yourself and your soul.

Connect with Leanne

Website: fengshuistoreandmore.com

The *Feng Shui Store and More* Facebook Page: facebook.com/Thefengshuistoreandmore

The new eBook Facebook group: facebook.com/groups/2717572748261232

Be sure to join my Newsletter! You can register at my website (above) if you have not already for updates each month on the Monthly Bagua Energy Map and also the Zodiac monthly charts. I will also have updates on all our webinars this year, and online courses.

Want your FREE 30 min Qi Chat on how we can support you and your home or office? Click this link:

calendly.com/thefengshuistoreandmore/feng-shui-qi-chat

Book in a time that works for you. This is also a chance for us to see if we are a fit for each other, and if you would like to go further with your Feng Shui Journey.

www.ingramcontent.com/pod-product-compliance
Lightning Source LLC
Chambersburg PA
CBHW071410290426
44108CB00014B/1756